MINERVA'S DREAM

Written by Katherine Mead
Illustrated by Jonathan Gregerson

STECK-VAUGHN®
C O M P A N Y

A Division of Harcourt Brace & Company

www.steck-vaughn.com

Contents

The Royal Family

nce upon a time, King Martin and Queen Margaret lived in a grand castle. It was in a very cold, icy land. They had three children. Their sons were Prince Eggbert and Prince Mortimer. Their daughter was Her Royal Highness, Princess Minerva. The royal family was very happy. Well, one person wasn't.

The king and queen loved their children very, very much. But they had some silly ideas about how boys and girls should act.

Prince Eggbert and Prince Mortimer had to be strong and brave. They learned to play sports and ride horses. What they loved to do most was to play hockey on the Royal Team. Every year their team played at the Royal Games.

Princess Minerva had to be kind and helpful. She learned to sew and cook. She was on the Royal Cooking Team. Princess Minerva did not like this at all. She wanted to play hockey. Why should only princes get to play hockey?

4

Prince Eggbert and Prince Mortimer played hockey all the time. They were very good at it. Rain or shine, they were both out on the ice practicing all day. Princess Minerva liked to watch them play.

One day Princess Minerva asked, "May I play hockey with you?"

"No!" they shouted. "A princess can't play hockey. Find something else to do."

Princess Minerva said, "How do you know that a princess can't play hockey? If you'd give me a chance, you'd see how good I could be."

"We'll believe it when we see it!" yelled her brothers.

That afternoon, Princess Minerva went to see King Martin. "Dad, I have a question. May I play hockey with Eggie and Mortie? I would be very good at it."

"No, Minnie, my sweet," said the king. "A princess can't play hockey. It's too rough for you. Why don't you sew a pretty dress?"

Princess Minerva sat down by the king. First she got out her royal needle and thread and her silver scissors. She found her golden yardstick and some purple material. Then she sewed a royal purple dress. She tried it on, but it was too short for a dress. Princess Minerva said to herself, "This looks more like a shirt. Hmmm, it would be perfect for ...."

9

Minerva's Plan

The next day Queen Margaret and Princess Minerva were in the kitchen. Minerva asked, "Please Mom, may I play hockey with Eggie and Mortie? I want to be the goalie!"

"Oh, no," said the queen, "a princess shouldn't play hockey. You might get hurt! Why don't you bake a royal cake?"

Princess Minerva got out the pots and pans. She stirred together some flour, chocolate, and butter. Then she mixed in some sand and glue! Princess Minerva baked the cake a bit too long. The cake was very small and hard when she took it out of the oven. Princess Minerva smiled and said to herself, "This cake would be perfect for ...."

10

11

The next day Princess Minerva went to see her grandfather in his art studio. "Grandfather," began Princess Minerva. "Do you think a princess should be able to play hockey?"

"Of course not, my dear Minerva. I've never seen a princess play hockey. That's a silly idea," said her grandfather. "Why don't you make something pretty out of this clay?"

Princess Minerva put on her apron. She got out the clay. Then she molded it and let it dry. It became very hard. It looked a bit like a big basket. Princess Minerva smiled and said to herself, "This basket would be perfect for ...."

Princess Minerva went to see her grandmother in the library. Her grandmother was reading a book about the royal family.

"Grandmother, do you think a princess can play hockey?" asked Princess Minerva.

"What? Play hockey? No, no, no. Why, in my day, a princess would never play hockey," said Grandmother. "Why don't you read a good book?"

Princess Minerva looked for a book. She got on the floor and read a book about playing hockey. Princess Minerva smiled to herself. Her eyes twinkled. She said, "Hmmm, I think I have everything I'll need ...."

15

The Royal Games

It was almost time for the Royal Games. Each year there were many games and races. Wonderful prizes were given to the winners. The grand prize was a trophy for the best hockey team. All the hockey teams wanted to win that prize. It was a golden hockey stick.

The teams practiced and practiced. They played hockey day and night. Hockey was the talk of the village. Well, almost everyone talked about hockey. Princess Minerva was very quiet.

17

"Who do you think will win the big game, my dears?" Queen Margaret asked her sons. It was just two days before the Royal Games.

"I'm sure we'll win," said Prince Mortimer and Prince Eggbert.

"The royal team must win!" said King Martin. "We just have to win the big game!"

"Who will be the goalie?" asked Princess Minerva. "Didn't you know that Oscar will be in the speed skating race at the same time?"

"She's right! We have to find a new goalie," said the king.

"Why don't you have tryouts tomorrow?" asked Princess Minerva.

The Tryouts

The tryouts were held the next day. Many players came to try out for goalie. This could be their big chance to play on the Royal Team. King Martin and his family watched the tryouts.

"What do you think, dear?" asked Queen Margaret. "They all seem good."

"Yes, but that small one in the funny mask is really the best. Look how he slaps out the puck," said the king.

"Yes, and he moves so quickly," said the queen. "He reminds me of someone, but I don't know who it is."

"He is the best goalie, so he shall play on the Royal Team!" said the king.

Later that day, the king said, "It's too bad you missed watching the tryouts, Minnie. The new goalie is very good. He's small, but strong. I do think he is one of the best players I've ever seen."

"He's so fast! He reminds me of someone I know. I'm not sure who it is," said the queen.

"Where did they find him?" asked Princess Minerva.

"I don't know. He just ran off saying he'd be back tomorrow for the game," said the king. "I hope he shows up."

"Oh, I'm sure he will," said Princess Minerva with a smile.

The Royal Games began. Many hockey teams came to play. In the final game, the Royal Team played against the Village Icers. The Royal Team won! King Martin started to give the trophy to the Royal Team. Just then the goalie took off his face mask and helmet. The goalie was Princess Minerva!

The crowd cheered, "Look! It's Princess Minerva!" Everyone clapped as she waved to the people.

From that day on, the Royal Hockey Team never played without their star goalie, Princess Minerva.